King Nebuchadnezzar's golden statue

Story by Penny Frank
Illustrated by Eric Ford

D0394578

Guideposts
26

CARMEL • NEW YORK 10512

The Bible tells us how God chose the Israelites to be his special people. He made them a promise that he would always love and care for them. But they must obey him.

This is the story of three Israelites who obeyed God even when they were prisoners in Babylon–a foreign country. You can find the story in your Bible in Daniel, chapters 1 to 3.

Copyright © 1984 Lion Publishing

Published by
Lion Publishing plc
Icknield Way, Tring, Herts, England
Lion Publishing Corporation
1705 Hubbard Avenue, Batavia,
Illinois 60510, USA
Albatross Books Pty Ltd
PO Box 320, Sutherland, NSW 2232, Australia

First edition 1984
Reprinted 1984, 1985, 1986, 1987

British Library Cataloguing in Publication Data

Frank, Penny
   King Nebuchadnezzar's golden statue. – (The Lion Story Bible; 26)
   1. Nebuchadnezzar, *King of Babylon* – Juvenile literature
   I. Title   II. Ford, Eric
   224'.509505   BS580.N4

Library of Congress Cataloging in Publication Data

1. Nebuchadnezzar II, King of Babylonia, d. 562 B.C.—Juvenile literature. 2. Babylonia—Kings and rulers—Biography—Juvenile literature. 3. Bible. O.T.—Biography—Juvenile literature. [1. Nebuchadnezzar II, King of Babylonia, d. 562 B.C. 2. Bible stories—O.T.] I. Ford, Eric, ill. II. Title. III. Series: Frank, Penny. Lion Story Bible; 26.
BS580.N4F73 1984   224'.509505
84-15511

Printed and bound in Hong Kong by Mandarin Offset Marketing (HK) Ltd
This Guideposts edition is published by special arrangement with Lion Publishing

King Nebuchadnezzar of Babylon won a great battle against the Israelites.

He brought back many people from Israel as prisoners to work for him in the city of Babylon.

King Nebuchadnezzar said to his chief servant, 'Go and talk to all the Israelite men I have brought to Babylon. Pick out the ones who are handsome and clever and strong. They will work in my palace.'

So the servant carefully chose the best Israelites. Four of the men he chose were friends already. They loved God. They were glad they were going to stay together.

The four friends were anxious when they were sent to the palace.

'We must serve God,' they said. 'What shall we do if we are given the wrong food to eat, food which is against God's laws?'

So one of the four friends, called
Daniel, went to talk to the chief servant.
   'We want to keep the laws God has
given us, even though we are in
Babylon,' he said.

'We are not allowed to eat the food you have prepared for us,' said Daniel. 'Please give us just vegetables and water for ten days. You will see that God will keep us healthy if we obey him.'

The chief servant said, 'I hope I don't get into trouble for this.'

After ten days the chief servant found
that the four friends were well and
strong.

'Your God does take care of you
when you keep his laws,' he said. He
was surprised.

One day there was great excitement in the palace. The king had had a bad dream.

The four friends heard him shouting at his wise men. 'What was the dream about? And what does it mean?' he yelled.

The wise men all came out looking very
worried.

'That's an impossible question,' they
said. 'How can we know what he
dreamed?'

The king shouted out after them,
'If you can't tell me, I'll have you all
killed.'

11

The wise men shook with fear.
But God showed Daniel
what the dream had been
and Daniel went in to tell
the king. 'I can tell you
what you dreamed. And
what it means,' he said.
The king listened carefully.

The king was very pleased with Daniel.
Then he said, 'Your God is great and
has made you clever. I want you to be
my special wise man. I will give your
friends important work too.'

King Nebuchadnezzar could see how powerful God was. He knew that God had made Daniel into a clever man.

But the king still thought that he was the most important person of all.

So King Nebuchadnezzar made
an enormous golden statue. The king
told everybody to come and see it.
There were big crowds of people.
A band was ready to play
music.

'When you hear the music, you must
bow down to my statue,' said the king.

A servant read the king's command.
'If you hear the music of the band
and see the golden statue and do not
bow down you will be thrown into
a blazing fire and burned to death.'

All the Israelites knew that their law said they must only bow down to God.

Daniel's three friends said, 'We love God. We cannot bow down to the golden statue.'

When King Nebuchadnezzar heard that Daniel's three friends were not bowing down to his golden statue he was very angry.

'If you do not bow down you will be thrown into the blazing fire,' he said.

'Maybe God will save us from the fire,'
said the three friends. 'And maybe he
won't. But anyway we cannot bow
down to the statue.'

King Nebuchadnezzar was furious.
'Heat the fire seven times hotter!' he
shouted.

'Tie them up and throw them into the
fire,' commanded the king.
The fire was so hot it burned the
men who threw the friends into the fire.

Then King Nebuchadnezzar's face went white. He said to his men, 'We put three men in the fire. But look: there are four now, and they are walking in the fire.'

The people screamed.

King Nebuchadnezzar shouted to the
men to come out of the fire. Only the
three friends came. They were not
burned. They did not even smell of fire.

King Nebuchadnezzar told all the people in Babylon, 'Now I know that the God of the Israelites is the true God. Because these three men obeyed him, he sent his angel to rescue them. There is no other God who can rescue like this.'

The Story Bible Series from Guideposts is made up of 50 individual stories for young readers, building up an understanding of the Bible as one story—God's story—a story for all time and all people.

The Old Testament story books tell the story of a great nation—God's chosen people, the Israelites—and God's love and care for them through good times and bad. The stories are about people who knew and trusted God. From this nation came one special person, Jesus Christ, sent by God to save all people everywhere.

The New Testament story books cover the life and teaching of God's Son, Jesus. The stories are about the people he met, what he did and what he said. Almost all we know about the life of Jesus is recorded in the four Gospels—Matthew, Mark, Luke and John. The word gospel means 'good news.'

The last four stories in this section are about the first Christians, who started to tell others the 'good news,' as Jesus had commanded them—a story which continues today all over the world.

The story of *King Nebuchadnezzar's golden statue* comes towards the end of the Old Testament, from the book of Daniel, chapters 1 to 3. Nebuchadnezzar, king of Babylon, had attacked Jerusalem and taken hostages back to his own land, together with treasure plundered from God's temple. Daniel and his friends were from the royal family and the nobility of Judah. Far from home, at the court of a foreign despot, they were still determined to serve and obey God, trusting him no matter what the danger. And, as the story shows, God was well able to take care of them.